A Bibliographical And Literary Account Of A Manuscript Hebrew Roll: Containing The Pentateuch

William Tite

In the interest of creating a more extensive selection of rare historical book reprints, we have chosen to reproduce this title even though it may possibly have occasional imperfections such as missing and blurred pages, missing text, poor pictures, markings, dark backgrounds and other reproduction issues beyond our control. Because this work is culturally important, we have made it available as a part of our commitment to protecting, preserving and promoting the world's literature. Thank you for your understanding.

A

BIBLIOGRAPHICAL AND LITERARY

ACCOUNT

OF A

MANUSCRIPT HEBREW ROLL,

CONTAINING

THE PENTATEUCH.

LONDON:
M.DCCC.LXIII.

[Not Published.]

A BIBLIOGRAPHICAL AND LITERARY ACCOUNT OF A MANUSCRIPT HEBREW ROLL OF THE PENTATEUCH.

THE Volume which is described in the ensuing pages, was purchased at the Sale of the Library of the late MANUEL F. JOHNSON, Esq. Radcliffe Observer at Oxford. It was sold on May 27th, 1862, by Messrs. Sotheby and Wilkinson, and was described in their Catalogue in the following terms:—

"Lot 57. MOSIS PENTATEUCHUS, HEBRAICÈ, CUM PUNCTIS: beautifully written on vellum as a Roll (47 feet in length, and 4¼ inches in breadth), on carved ivory rollers, with carved ivory Hand as a Pointer, and Cover of embroidery of silk, gold and silver threads, enclosed in a mahogany Ark, with embroidered Veil. One of the most elegant Hebrew Rolls ever offered for sale."

Although the bibliographical description of a Hebrew Roll is usually very concise and unattractive, it is not because the subject is in itself intrinsically destitute of interest, but really because there is seldom any attempt made to make it otherwise. To an intelligent Jew this neglect is not of any consequence; but intellectual or religious persons of the Christian faith, will find both interest and sympathy in looking at a Hebrew Roll, when they are informed of something more than the title of it, even though the appearance of the characters may be repulsive to them, and the language quite unknown. Under the impression of these considerations, it is proposed to give such a literary account of the fine volume of the Pentateuch procured from Mr. Johnson's Library, as may serve to exhibit some of the many points of interest which it contains common to all such as read and regard The Holy Scriptures. The collation, also, which is here given, may possibly be found useful as a guide to any other Manuscript Roll of the Five Books of Moses; but the volume now to be described is more than usually complete in all its appointments, though it never could have belonged to any synagogue.

It is of course very generally known, that *the Hebrew Sacred Books of the Law* which are used in public worship, are manuscripts; and that they are not of the ordinary square form, but are wound round *Umbilici*, or rollers, in the manner of the Roman volumes: excepting that the Hebrew writings are rolled from both ends, and meet in the centre. They have, however, several peculiarities, proper to such records only; some account of which may very appropriately precede any statement of the contents of this Roll, as supplying a general description of its external features.

All copies of *The Law* must be transcribed from ancient manuscripts of approved character only (Note I. p. 23), in the old square letter, with pure ink, and on parchment prepared for the express purpose by a Jew, who is neither a heretic nor a Samaritan, from the skin of a clean animal (Note II. p. 24). The different membranes of the roll are to be secured to each other by fine thread, spun by a Jewess, or by ligatures, also taken from the sinews of clean animals; and every membrane must contain a certain number of columns of prescribed dimensions, each consisting of a certain number of lines and words (Note III. p. 25). None of the words may be written with points, or by memory, or without being first pronounced by the transcriber; and the

Name of God is not to be written but with great devotion and attention, and the pen should be washed before writing it. The want of a single letter, or the redundancy of a single letter; the writing of prose as verse (*open*) or verse as prose (*close*), will all be sufficient to vitiate a manuscript: and, when a copy has been completed, it must be examined and corrected within thirty days afterwards, to determine whether it shall be received or rejected. If the transcript should be approved, there is usually a certificate to that effect added at the end: and, as the presentation of such a copy of the Law to a synagogue is regarded as an act of merit, the name of the donor is included in the subscription. The present Roll, however, terminates with the end of the Book of Deuteronomy, *excepting that the Last Three Words of it have never been written.* It is therefore certain that this volume has never been examined or presented; though there does not appear to be any reason for supposing it to be otherwise than correct. The writing was probably executed in Holland, in the early part of the last century; and it is uniformly good, but not all equally excellent. There are not any points in it, though the title in the catalogue of the sale whence it was purchased contains the words *cum punctis*; but there are many instances of letters in proper names surmounted with *apices*, or ornaments like horns or plumes, which are not admitted into the most orthodox manuscripts.

The whole extent of this Roll appears to be about 47 feet 3 inches; and it is composed of Fifty-one separate Membranes, sewed together, measuring 4¾ inches in depth. The writing is in a small, rough, square character, in columns 3¼ inches in height, by one inch and five-eighths in breadth; each containing forty-two lines, quite filled up: but the parchment has been ruled for one line more. The initial and concluding words of each book do not differ from the rest of the writing, but at the end of each book, the space of four lines is left before the commencement of the next. The several skins are all remarkably white and fine, soft and substantial, almost like stout white kid leather; but they vary in length, from nearly 16 inches to 6¼ inches; and the number of columns written on them is from three to seven; though in a single instance there are eight. A collation of the particular extent of the several books is given in the following list:—

    I. GENESIS — *Berashith* — In the Beginning — *Membranes 1-14, ending on Column 65.*

    II. EXODUS — *Shemoth* — The Names — *Membr. 14-24, ending on Col. 55.*

    III. LEVITICUS — *Vaikra* — And He called — *Membr. 24-32, ending on Col. 40.*

    IV. NUMBERS — *Bemeedibar* — In the Wilderness — *Membr. 32-42, ending on Col. 58.*

    V. DEUTERONOMY — *Alehe Debarim* — These are the Words — *Membr. 42-51, ending on Col. 49.*

There cannot be a doubt, however fastidiously scrupulous the regulations for transcribing these Rolls may be regarded in modern times,—that the religious observance of them, which has continued undisputed for so many centuries, has been providentially employed as one effectual means of preserving the purity of the Pentateuch. Out of the careful practice of distinguishing between the writing of prose and verse, arises also one very interesting feature which may be noticed in this Roll; since the great poetical compositions occurring in the early books of the Scriptures, are thus made manifest to the sight of all, even when the characters of the language are unknown. The Pentateuch likewise contains many other passages of interest, not easily to be distinguished in such a manuscript as the present, but which are capable of being readily pointed out by a very simple system of reference. *Firstly, therefore, all the Membranes, or skins, of the volume, are Numbered, on the plan of the English Record Rolls of the Middle-ages; commencing with the Book of Genesis, at the right hand end, and continuing in one series to the close of Deuteronomy. These divisions are lightly marked in red at the upper right hand of each skin; and, after the end of the first book, there is added the particular numeral of the membrane of every following book in its order. The Columns are numbered below for every book separately.*—(Note IV. page 26.) The method of reference having been thus explained, a few of the most interesting passages in each of the Five Books of Moses may now be noticed; and it is evident that the same system may be employed for the illustration of any other Hebrew Roll, if there should not be any objection to marking it.

I. GENESIS.

The first remarkable passage in this volume, is the genealogical account of the descendants of Noah, by whom all the Nations were divided in the earth after the Flood. In the printed text of the Holy Scriptures this passage occurs in chap. x. and xi., and on this Roll it commences on *Membrane* 3, *with the last three lines of Column* 11, *and the whole of Column* 12. The many proper names contained in this part of the text will probably very easily be distinguished.

The Call of Abraham, as related in chap. xii. of the printed text, will also be found on *Column* 12.

The narrative of the trial of the faith of Abraham in the command given to him to offer up Isaac, as related in chap. xxii. of the printed text, is written on *Membrane* 6, *Column* 28. It is recited daily, in the early part of every morning-service. Ishmael's alienation of the birthright is on *Column* 29; and the account of the artifice of Rebekah and Jacob for obtaining the blessing of Isaac, chap. xxvii. of the printed text, is on *Column* 31.

On *Membrane* 7, *Column* 33, is written the narrative of the Vision of Jacob at Beth-El, printed text chap. xxviii. 10, and in the last word of the column it will be seen that a single character, (ד *Daleth*) is elongated to a very unusual length, being equal to nearly three words in the preceding line, though one of them is written with an extended letter. In Hebrew writing it is never permitted that a word should be divided; and therefore several of the letters may be extended for the purpose of filling up a line, or for distinguishing a name, a title, or an important expression. In the present instance it is possible that the transcriber desired to make the last word in his copy of this column agree with that in the original manuscript, since the word itself—*Gnemodi*—" and will keep me"—is not generally distinguished. The greater part of the Patriarch's vow occupies the upper lines of column 34.

At this particular part of the Roll, to the end of Genesis, the ordinary separation of the book becomes extremely difficult to identify; and the divisions of the chapters of the printed text must be sought for in the half lines of close columns, or of long and unbroken paragraphs. For weekly reading in the synagogue, the Five Books of Moses are divided into Fifty-four sections, (סְדָרִים), the arrangement of which is called *Sedraim*, a Syriac word, with a Hebrew termination, meaning the Order or Series, one of which constitutes the First Lesson every Sabbath-day; and each section is again separated into seven portions, one of which is read to one of seven other persons, who are called up to the altar to hear them.[1] The *Printed* Hebrew Bibles contain both of these divisions—chapters and sections—properly numbered; but in the present Roll there are not any distinctive marks attached to the sections and paragraphs.—There are to be found, however, so many proper names of persons and places in all the early books of The Holy Scriptures, that they will generally assist in the identification of any passage in the Law; and, therefore, even in the dense mass of writing at the latter part of the first book of this Roll, may be recognised the prophetical and poetical blessing of the dying Jacob, as contained in chap. xlix. of the printed text. It occurs on *Membrane* 14, and it occupies *Columns* 62 to 65. With the first five lines on column 65 the book of Genesis is completed in this manuscript.

II. Exodus.

After a blank of four lines, the Second Book of Moses commences on the present Roll: and it contains two very striking passages which cannot fail of exciting interest when they are pointed out. The first is the Song of Moses and the Israelites, after the destruction of the Egyptians in the Red Sea: chap. xv. 1-19 of the printed text; which, being written as verse uttered by different voices, is very easy to be recognised and understood. The other remarkable passage contains the Decalogue, as it appears in the printed text, chap. xx. 1-14, and the several Commandments are distinguished in this manuscript by small red Roman Numerals. It will be found on *Membrane* 19, *Column* 25.

The Song of Moses is written on *Membrane* 18, *Column* 19, and it exhibits, by the peculiar arrangement of the lines, the dialogue form in which it was probably chaunted. There cannot be a doubt that all the Poetry of the ancient Hebrews was regularly

---

[1] " Give a Portion to *Seven*, and also to *Eight*, for thou knowest not what evil shall be upon the earth." *Eccles.* xi. 2.

2 A.

(Membr. 18, Col. 19.   Addition to page 9.)

G UNTO THE LORD, AND SPAKE,
ED GLORIOUSLY: The horse
⅃   ² The Lord is my strength and my song,
⅃ation.   The God
(³ The Lord is a Man of War: The Lord
⅃o the sea.   His chosen
(s have covered them, and they sank to the bottom, as
⅃power: Thy right hand,
(greatness of Thine excellency Thou hast overthrown
Them as stubble.   ⁸ And with the blast
(And upright, like an heap stood
⅃the sea.   ⁹ Then said
⅃   I will divide the spoil; full of them shall be
⅃em.   ¹⁰ Thou didst blow
⅃   They sank as lead in the waters
Hs?   Who
⅃   Fearful in praises, doing
⅃wallowed them.   ¹³ Thou hast led forth
⅃hast guided them in Thy strength unto the habitation
(Sorrow
⅃   ¹⁵ Then shall be amazed the leaders
(hold upon them: And melt away
⅃   ¹⁶ Upon them shall fall fear
⅃s still as a stone,   Until
⅃   Until that People pass over
⅃e Mountain of Thine inheritance.   In the place
⅃   In the Sanctuary which hath been established
⅃ER.   ¹⁹ For
⅃ And THE LORD brought again upon them the waters
(In the Midst of the Sea.

rhythmical, though the rules by which their verses were composed are certainly now unknown. It was also often antiphonal, or responsive; as the passage which is now referred to, with many others, indisputably indicate; and that it was made up of similar, or balanced, sentences, in the nature of proverbs,—generally called parallelisms,—seems to be the chief distinguishing characteristic of Hebrew verse, and is nearly the only feature of it which is commonly admitted at the present time; after all the investigation and learning which have been devoted to the subject.

The very artificial and expressive arrangement of the Song of Moses and the Children of Israel, as it is here written, and as it is always printed in Hebrew, seems intended visibly to exhibit the manner in which it was alternately chaunted or sung; and the same order is also followed in the triumphal song of Deborah and Barak, after the destruction of Sisera, *Judges*, chap. v. This peculiar arrangement may first be shewn by the following diagram:

In this figure the first line represents the prose passage in which the song is introduced, "Then Sang Moses and the children of Israel This Song unto the Lord, and spake:" the word "saying" is represented by the short dash at the *right hand* of the next line; and the commencement by Moses, "I will Sing unto the Lord for He hath triumphed gloriously," is shewn by the long rule in the centre. The second short dash on the left, stands for the words "the horse," the remainder of the sentence being completed by the right hand rule of the next line. The written passages of the Roll, therefore, appear to express the verses of the poem as given forth by Moses, standing between two large bodies of the Israelites, and the intervening spaces the repetition of them by all the tribes; whilst the imperfect verses at the beginning and ending of each line, seem to indicate the unceasing succession of the song being carried on until it was finished. In the very close condensation of the Hebrew, there is not any difficulty in compressing the several verses into these short spaces; but all translations are unavoidably more or less diffuse than the original, and thus the visible measure becomes lost. An attempt, however, has been made on another page to exhibit the English version of the song arranged in the Hebrew order, but the irregularity occasioned by the difference of the languages cannot be entirely overcome. In those editions of the Authorised Version of the Holy Scriptures in which the poetical parts are distinguished from the prose, the verses of this song are printed only as separate paragraphs. This passage of Scripture is included in the daily morning-service of the synagogue, and also in that for the morning of the Sabbath.

The Book of Exodus is completed on *Column* 55, *Membrane* 11, of the present Roll: and after a space of four lines are written the first seven lines of the next. The writing of the whole book occupies somewhat more than nine membranes.

III. Leviticus.

This portion of the Law also extends through nine skins of the volume, and it terminates on *Membrane* 32, *Column* 40. The usual blank of four lines is left at the end of it, and the same column contains likewise five lines of the next book. The most remarkable passage in Leviticus which may be noticed in the present Roll, is the section containing the Blessing pronounced on the faithful Israelites, and the Curse on such as should break the Commandments, chap. xxvi. of the printed text,—which will be found on *Membrane* 31, *Columns* 37 to 39.

IV. Numbers.

The text of this book extends through 11 skins and 58 columns of manuscript: and it contains many passages of the greatest importance, though they are not in general such as are very characteristic externally. In the first four columns, however, on *Membrane* 33, may be observed the official returns made to Moses, in execution of the command given to number the tribes of Israel, written in short paragraphs, and easily to be distinguished by the many proper names occurring in them. After these may be noticed the solemn and eloquent Form of Blessing which the priests were appointed to use to bless the children of Israel, chap. vi. 22–27 of the printed text, written as a separate paragraph on *Membrane* 34, *Column* 12. It is pronounced in all the daily morning-services of the synagogue. *On the succeeding*

Column of Membrane 34, commencing with the third line, appears the catalogue of the offerings of the princes of the twelve tribes for the dedication of the altar of the tabernacle, chap. vii. 12–88 of the printed text; and it extends to column 16 on the following skin. In this book also, and nearly at this part of it, occurs the last section of the solemn and indispensable office of the daily devotion of the Jews called *Shema;* being that portion of the text which appoints a fringe of remembrance to be added to the ordinary garments. It forms the last paragraph of *Column* 27 *on Membrane* 34, and in the printed versions it is contained in chap. xv. 37–41; but the most important passages of it belong to the ensuing book. In the subsequent parts of the Book of Numbers, the following references include the most interesting and remarkable subjects.

On *Membrane* 36, *Columns* 22, 23, is the list of those persons whom Moses sent to search the Land of Canaan, chap. xiii. 4–16 of the printed text; and on *Membrane* 38, *Columns* 37–40, is written the narrative relating to Balak and Balaam, as contained in chap. xxii–xxiv. of the printed text. It will be observed that however poetical is the language of the Prophet, it was not regular Hebrew verse, but appears in the continuous form of prose. On *Membrane* 41, *Columns* 53,54, is recorded the itinerary of the forty-two journeys of the Israelites in the wilderness, chap. xxxiii. 1–49 of the printed text; and on the same skin, *Column* 55, beginning at the tenth line from the bottom, are the names of those whom God appointed to divide the promised land, chap. xxxiv. 16–29 of the Authorised Version.

V. Deuteronomy.

The writing of this portion of the Law commences on *Membrane* 42, *Column* 58, after a blank of four lines: but the arrangement of the manuscript at this place differs entirely from that of all the other parts of it in respect of the same divisions, as the space occurs in the middle of the column, between two paragraphs of 19 lines each. In this invaluable book are contained many passages of the highest interest and importance, but in a Hebrew Roll few of them would be attractive or even evident to ordinary sight. Two of those parts which are the most esteemed by the

Jews, are the sentences forming the first two sections of the daily personal service of every religious Jew, called *Kiriath Shema*, or the Reading of the *Shema*, chap. vi. 4–9, xi. 13–21, of the printed text. The first will be found on *Membrane* 44, *Column* 11, of this Roll, and it may easily be distinguished by the large size of the character ע *Ain*, at the end of the commencing word *Shema*, Hear: whence the office derives its name. It is that pre-eminent ordinance of the Law, which is referred to by Jesus Christ as being " the first and great commandment" (*Matth.* xxii. 37; *Mark*, xii. 29, 30) —" HEAR, O ISRAEL, THE LORD OUR GOD IS ONE LORD. And thou shalt love the Lord thy God, with all thine heart, and with all thy soul, and with all thy might. And THESE WORDS, which I command thee this day, shall be in thine heart. And thou shalt teach them diligently unto thy children; and shalt talk of them when thou sittest in thine house, and when thou walkest by the way, and when thou liest down, and when thou risest up." The second paragraph of the *Shema* is less visible than the first in this manuscript, but it is written on *Membrane* 45, *Column* 18. The *Kiriath Shema*, in an extended form, is included in all the synagogue-services.

In these two passages are contained the authority for wearing the *Phylactery* on the forehead, and the *Tephillin* on the hand, during the act of prayer; for affixing the *Mezzuza* in door-ways; and for the daily reading of those parts of the Law in which they are commanded, with the passage from the book of *Numbers* relating to the memorial-fringes. Thou " shalt talk of them," says the ordinary printed text of *Deuteronomy*, vi. 7–9, " when thou sittest in thine house, and when thou walkest by the way, and when thou liest down, and when thou risest up. And thou shalt bind them for a sign upon thine hand, and they shall be as frontlets between thine eyes. And thou shalt write them upon the posts of thy house, and on thy gates." Maimonides has very properly defined night and morning to be the meaning of the words " when thou liest down, and when thou risest up:" and therefore the evening reading of the *Shema* might take place from the time of the appearance of the stars until midnight; after which it ought not to be delayed, though a person might not then retire to rest. In the morning, the recital might be made from the dawn to the third hour of the day (3 o'clock to 9), or the time when the morning-sacrifice was appointed to be offered.

TH...

Columns 46, 47.

AND MOSES SPAKE IN THE EAR... SONG,

Verse 1 Give ear, O ye Heavens, and I will sp... mouth.
2 My doctrine shall drop as the rain, ...
 As the small rain upon the tender herb...
3 Because I will call upon The Name of...
4 He is The Rock. His work is perfect...
 A God of Truth, and without iniquity...
5 They have corrupted themselves: th... ...ration.
6 Do ye thus requite THE LORD? ...
 Is not He thy Father that hath gotten... ...hed thee?
7 Remember the days of old; ... ...ons:
 Ask thy Father, and he will shew thee...
8 When The Most High divided to the N... ...m,
 He set the bounds of The People ... ...ldren of Israel.
9 For the Portion of THE LORD is His I...
... For their vine is of the vine of Sodom...
 Their grapes are grapes of gall, ...
13 Their wine is the poison of dragons, ...
14 Is not this laid up in store with Me? ...
15 To Me belongeth vengeance and recom...
 For the day of their calamity is at han... ...them make haste."
36 For THE LORD shall judge His people, ...
 When He seeth that their power is gon...
37 And He shall say "Where are their go...
38 Which did eat the fat of their sacrifices... ...fferings;
 Let them rise up and help you, ...
39 See now, THAT I, EVEN I, AM HE! ...
 I kill, and I make alive; ...
 Neither is there any that can deliver ou...
 And say—I LIVE FOR EVER. ...
 And Mine hand take hold on judgmen... ...mies,
 And will reward them that hate Me. ... blood,
 And My sword shall devour flesh, ... and of the captives,
 From the beginning of revenges upon t... ...ple:
 For He will avenge the blood of His a... ...versaries.
 AND WILL BE MERCIFUL UNTO HIS LAN...

One of the most important passages in the present part of this Roll is the repetition of the Decalogue, as it appears in chap. v. 6–18 of the printed text. It will be found on *Membrane* 44, *Column* 10; and the several Commandments are indicated by small red Roman numerals, as they are also in the parallel passage in Exodus.

On *Membranes* 48, 49, *Columns* 37, 38, may be recognised the short separate sentences of the curses pronounced on Mount Ebal, as contained in chap. xxvii. 14–26 of the printed text, and in the Commination Service of the Church of England. The general repetition of blessings and curses comprised in chap. xxvii. is written in the close matter of *Columns* 38–41.

At the close of the volume appears another of the most interesting passages contained in it, and it is one also which is perceptible and attractive to general observation from the peculiar manner in which it is written. It is the last song uttered by Moses before he ascended Mount Pisgah to die, as recited in chap. xxii. of the printed text, and it will be found on *Membrane* 51, *Columns* 46, 47, of the Roll, in the form of two narrow parallel columns of 35 short lines each. The appearance of this composition in the manuscript is represented by the following diagram; and on another page an attempt has been made to give the Hebrew arrangement with the English version, though with but indifferent success.

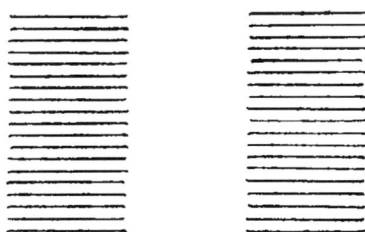

Though the external appearance of this magnificent Poem differs from that of The Song at the Red Sea, it will probably soon be observed that the principle of parallelisms and continuous recital is the same in both. Here, also, the single speaker seems to be placed in the centre of two large masses of the tribes, and to turn and address himself alternately to each; dividing the beginning, the continuation, and the conclusion, of his sublime verses between them. *In this manner, therefore, the annexed attempt to express the English version of this song in the Hebrew order must be read across;* as the two columns form but one verse, like the old English measure of unbroken Iambics, which subsequently gave way to stanzas of eight and six syllables. The principle may be further illustrated by the following rude effort to render the first lines of this noble composition into the verse in question, the separation, or breathing-place, being indicated by a dash:

> Give ear, ye Heavens, and I will speak—And let Earth hear me too:
> My teachings shall as rain descend—my speech shall flow as dew;
> Like small rain on the tender herb—or showers upon the sod:
> For I will call upon the Lord—And ye shall praise our God.

On Column 48 commences the solemn and eloquent Blessing of the Twelve Tribes by the departing Moses, the whole of which is poetical language of the highest order; but it is written in the consolidated form of prose, and therefore does not appear to be regarded as having been delivered in regular Hebrew verse. These passages, however, are all printed as verse, in the edition of the Holy Scriptures published by Mr. John Reeves in 1801, in which all the poetical parts are so distinguished, though without any authority being given for the variation. In all the ordinary Hebrew Bibles this part of the text is printed as prose.

After these passages follows the short narrative of the prophet's death, as related in chap. xxxiv. of the printed text; and the volume then terminates with a column of 41 lines quite full, and one left entirely blank for the addition of the three concluding words of Deuteronomy, whenever the Roll should be completed and appropriated to the use of a synagogue or of an individual.

Though the presentation of a manuscript copy of the Law to a synagogue is regarded as a meritorious act, yet the transcript, after it has been completed and approved, still requires to be made up into a perfect Roll, with all the proper external appointments belonging to it: most of which may be regarded as similar to the binding of a book for the service of a Christian church. The first of these equipments were the ROLLERS, round which one end of each of the extreme skins was to be folded and sewed. There is probably little doubt that these were originally two natural wooden cylinders,—or parts of round branches of trees,—until the importation of ivory by Solomon introduced it as a more costly and valuable material—as appears to be expressed in the name by which those rollers are still known—" *The Trees of Life*":—the probable origin of which is explained in the following manner.

The duty of unrolling and rolling up the volumes of the Law; carrying them in procession round the synagogue; holding them up above the altar, so as they might be seen by the whole congregation; and reading certain lessons from them on certain days; with other public services;—may all be executed by any Israelite, and are all esteemed to be especially honourable and meritorious. When these offices become vacant, the privilege of performing them was formerly offered to public auction in the synagogue by one of the clerks (Note V. page 27); and the funds which they produced were employed for the support of that church, and the relief of the poor belonging to it. In wealthy congregations, these sums were occasionally very considerable; and Buxtorf states that the privilege of unrolling and rolling up the Law, and elevating the open volumes before the people, was eagerly bought by the younger Jews in Germany. They considered, he says, that the very handling of the bands by which the books are tied, and the rollers, as " the Trees of Life," would make them wise and prosperous, preserve their health and extend their lives. And this belief is considered to be founded on sufficient authority in the literal meaning of the text in *Proverbs*, iii. 18, which refers to Wisdom, or the Knowledge of the Divine Law—" *She is a Tree of Life to them that Lay Hold upon Her; and happy is every one that Holdeth her Up*:" (עֵץ חַיִּים a Tree of Lives.)

In the present instance these Rollers are of substantial and very white ivory, about 10 inches in length, and are covered with carved ornaments on all the visible parts. The handles are nearly 2½ inches long, and the four broad disks above them, intended for the support and protection of the Rolls, are of about the same measure in diameter, and they are fluted and ornamented on their exterior surfaces. At the top of each roller is carved a large imperial crown, expressive of the name for this part of the cylinders, כתר התורה *Cathar Hathorath*, or " the Crown of the

Law."² In some of the more costly Rolls which have been presented to the principal synagogues by wealthy persons, these ornaments are made of silver-gilt, in the form of crowns, pomegranates, or trees hung with small bells. Picart has engraved a very fine example of a large Roll, with all its proper coverings and ornaments, in which the peculiarities and decorations referred to in these notices may all be recognised. It probably belonged to the great synagogue at Amsterdam. (*Cérémonies et Coûtumes Réligieuses*, i. p. 139.)

It has been already stated that in transcribing a copy of the Law, there should not be any word of it written from memory only, or without being first pronounced by the writer. The same principle of precision is observed also in the *Reading* of the Law and other sacred books, and an instrument is appointed to be used for regulating the reader, called the י *Yod*, or Hand, which is to be placed on every word of the Roll as it is uttered. This pointer is usually made of carved ivory, and consists of a stem terminating in the form of a hand, having three fingers folded down, and one extended, pointing to the word on which it is laid. The *Yod* belonging to the present Roll is of this description, being of ivory ornamented with carving, 6¼ inches in length, terminating at the lower end in a ring, to be put on over the forefinger of the reader; and at the other extremity in a short arm and hand with one finger extended. The pointer attached to the most valuable Rolls is frequently made of silver gilt, and the index-finger is ornamented with a gold ring containing a diamond.

At some distance from the place where the right hand and left hand Rolls meet in a volume of the Law, there is extended over the outside of it a piece of ornamented or figured silk; which Buxtorf says was commonly worked by some of the most skilful females of the synagogue; who also frequently embroidered the

---

² Buxtorf says that the two round pieces of wood to which the volume of the Law is attached, and on which it is wound, as used by the Jews in their Synagogues, are called בָּמוֹת (*Bamuth*), because they are elevated, and stand up high above the Roll; for which he cites the *Aruch* and the *Gemara*. The Crowns of the Law would therefore strictly be the ornaments mounted on the tops of these rollers. *Lexicon Chaldaicum, Talmudicum, et Rabbinicum* Basil. 1630. fol. col. 316.

mantle in which the Roll was inclosed: these being regarded as pious and meritorious works. In putting on this covering, the piece of silk is first to be completely extended; the opened Roll as it has been read is laid upon it; and, when the book is to be shut, the two ends of the silk are to be turned over each of the Rolls, which are then wound up and brought together, carrying the silk covering along with them. When, therefore, the book is closed, both the outside and inside of it are covered for some distance from the place of opening. The original intention of this wrapper was evidently to preserve the manuscript from dust or soil, both when it was closed and when it lay open to be read: but it seems also to represent the covering in which a complete copy of the Law was folded up; which Lightfoot, on Rabbinical authority, calls "The Cloth of the Quintanes." (Note VI. page 28.) In plainer language, this was " the Wrapper of the Five Books;" but the same passage also indicates that a similar covering, having a distinguishing name, was used for folding up all the other Rolls of the Holy Scriptures. A passage in the *Mishna* (*Meguillah*, iii. 1), which is given at length on another page, shews that these wrappers were of linen; and were called מִטְפַּחַת *Mitpachath*, a cloak. The Wrapper belonging to this Roll is 5¾ inches deep, and nearly 6 feet in length, but it is put on doubled. It is of plain crimson silk, with one edge of it hemmed and the other of the natural selvage.

For securing the volume thus made up, there is a Band, also of crimson silk, 4 feet 2½ inches long, and 2 inches broad, one end of which is formed into two ties. It is simply called קֶשֶׁר *Keshed*, a band or tie; and it is to be wound round the lower part of the volume, over both the Rolls, until the two separated ends are reached, which are then divided and tied in the usual way.

It is quite possible that when these equipments, which are all still proper to a Roll of the Law, were originally appointed, that there were some sacred, as well as appropriate meanings intended by them; which do not now appear to be remembered, though most of the names have been preserved. The outside covering of a Roll was anciently a cloth of fine linen, and in later times an embroidered canopy made like a tent, perforated in the roof with two openings for the upper ends of the rollers to pass through; to which Buxtorf gives the name of מפא *Mappa*, or the Mantle. Under such canopies the sacred books are still preserved in the Arks of the respective synagogues; and they are also carried beneath them in procession round the building on the Feast of the Law. The Mantle belonging to this volume is of Chinese gold and silver brocade, with coloured flowers; it is edged with a fringe of yellow silk; and it measures 9 inches in height, and 5½ inches across at the widest part at the bottom.

Long before Moses had written the books of the Ceremonial Law, a sacred depository had been made, in which was first placed the Decalogue, as it existed from the time when it was originally given and recorded on the tables of stone. At length, when all " the commandments, the statutes, and the judgments," had been received, and declared to the Tribes of Israel, Moses wrote the words of the Law in a Book, until they were finished; and gave the precious record to the Levites, directing them to " put it in the side," *or by the side*, of the Ark (Note VII. page 29) of the Covenant of the Lord their God, that it might be there for a witness against them (*Deut.* xxxi. 26). This Ark was made of shittim, or acacia, wood, in the form of an oblong chest or case, as the word אָרוֹן (*Aron*) really implies: " Two cubits and a half shall be the length thereof, and a cubit and a half the breadth thereof, and a cubit and a half the height thereof." In modern English measurement this would be a box of 3 feet 9 inches, by 2 feet 3 inches, and 2 feet 3 inches in depth; and its form and dimensions may readily be recognised in the feretories and portable shrines of the Middle-ages, which were also carried about by staves passing through rings placed at the sides. It may be further observed, that these reliquaries were frequently covered with gold plates decorated with jewels, the origin of which may be referred to the command, " thou shalt overlay it with pure gold, within and without shalt thou overlay it, and shalt make upon it a crown of gold round about." (*Exod.* xxv. 10–15.) It seems probable that the Ark was removed when Manasseh " set a carved image, the idol which he had made, in the House of God," (2 *Chron.* xxxiii. 7); and that, when it was replaced by Josiah (chap. xxxv. 3), the Book of the Law then discovered, might possibly have been found preserved within it, even 820 years after the time when it was originally deposited beside it. But all the recorded information concerning that discovery is, that the volume *was* found in the house of the Lord, by Hilkiah the priest, when "they brought out the money that was brought into the House of the Lord," (chap. xxxiv. 14); and this was contained in the perforated treasure-chest provided by Jehoiada the priest, 250 years before. It stood "beside the altar, on the right side as one cometh into the house of the Lord," (2 *Kings*, xii. 9); and perhaps the book might have been secured in this treasury by some pious priest, where it remained safe, though forgotten, during the half century which intervened between the reigns of Manasseh and Josiah.

About thirty years after the latter period, the greater part of the nation was carried away captive to Babylon: but before that event the copies of the Law and other sacred books appear to have been considerably increased; no doubt by the efforts of Josiah and Hilkiah to transcribe and preserve them. It is certain that Daniel and others of the Hebrew captives possessed some of those books; and the pious patriotism of Ezra seems to have led him to devote himself to the studying and copying of the Law, and also to engage in the same duties those other devout priests and Levites who are named in his history. In the last ages of the Second Temple, therefore, there must have been many volumes preserved there and employed in the daily services, but it is very doubtful whether that building contained an Ark in which they might be deposited. It is not unlikely that the sacred rolls were kept, each being wrapped up in its own proper linen cloth, in some such circular cases as those used by the Romans for their volumes, called *Capsæ* and *Scrinii*, which would allow of their separation into their proper subjects. These cases, or the several rolls, must also have been carefully preserved in some safe and appropriate place, possibly in the priests' ward, or the treasury; but it is remarkable that in all the particular account which Lightfoot gives of the different apartments of the Temple from Rabbinical authors, he does not indicate any place as being assigned to the sacred books.

In all the modern synagogues of the Jews there is a large recess formed at the extremity, the pavement of which is slightly elevated, having in the lower part a spacious cabinet or bookcase, enclosed with solid doors, wherein are placed the Rolls, each being wrapped up, tied, and covered with its own embroidered mantle.³ This part of the recess is properly called "The Ark," and before it is suspended an embroidered curtain, of velvet or other rich material, representing the פָּרֹכֶת (*Perekuth*) or "Veil of blue, and purple, and scarlet, and fine twisted linen of curious work with cherubims," (*Exod.* xxvi. 31). Whenever the camp set forward, Aaron and his sons came and took down the covering veil, and with it covered the Ark of the Testimony; over which they placed another wrapper of badgers' skins, and then a blue cloth (*Numbers*, iv. 5, 6.) In all the representations of this part of a synagogue engraved by Picart in the early part of the last century, the Arks appear like plain, close, lofty bookcases or wardrobes; and the cabinet made to contain the present Roll is of a precisely similar description. It is of mahogany, and in the external measurement it is 1 foot 2 inches in height from the feet to the top of the surmounting ornament; 7 inches wide, and 4 inches deep. It is enclosed with locked folding doors; and immediately beneath the ornamental top is a stout brass wire, on which hangs a veil or curtain 11½ inches in length, made of Chinese silver brocade like the material of the mantle within, bordered with a fringe of yellow silk. When the case is to be opened, this Veil should be drawn aside to the right hand. The interior measurement of the case, is as nearly as possible in the proportion of one-fourth of the dimensions appointed for the Ark; being 10⅞ inches in height, 6½ inches wide, and 4½ inches deep.

Before closing these notices of a Hebrew Roll of the Law, it should be remembered that there is a very curious illustration of the value of such a book contained in the Treatise of *The Mishna* which is called *Meguillah*, Chap. III. sect. 1. The principal subject of that interesting tract relates to the times and manner of reading "the Roll of the Book of Esther" at the Feast of *Purim*; but a considerable part of it is occupied with incidental matters, referring to the regulations of synagogues and public readings of the

---

³ Bruzen De la Martinière, apparently citing Buxtorf, calls this depository *Hechal*, without giving the Hebrew. The word no doubt is הֵיכָל (*Hecol*), The Temple, or the Sanctuary of the Temple; and also the Tabernacle, before the Temple was built. *Cérémon. Rélig.* I. p. 125.

Law. The rule in disposing of ecclesiastical property is, that the *money received for it must be applied to the purchase of something having a higher degree of sanctity than the article which has been sold.* " The inhabitants of a town," says the *Meguillah,* " who have sold the open square of the town, may for that money buy a Synagogue. The money obtained by the sale of a Synagogue, they may apply to the purchase of an Ark (for receiving the Rolls of the Holy Law). For the money obtained by the sale of such an Ark, Mantles or Wrappers for the Rolls of the Holy Law may be purchased. For the produce of such wrappers, Sacred Books (not of the Law) may be bought. For the price of Sacred Books, a Roll of the Holy Law may be procured; but, if a Roll of the Holy Law have been sold, it will not be lawful to employ *that money,* even for the purchase of other sacred books."

The only remaining subject which I have to notice, relates to that very remarkable apparatus of computations known by the name of the Masoretic Notes. In addition to all the minute observances for the transcription of the Law which I have already stated, I am disposed to regard these extraordinary memoranda to be really proofs of the extreme care of the Jews to secure and hold fast the literal text of The Holy Scriptures. Without attempting to give you in this place any history of the Masorites, or their works, I may state in general terms, that those who were so called of the later period counted the number of verses and letters in all the Sacred Books, and ascertained and recorded the middle verse and number in each. A full account of these Masoretic Notes will be found printed in Bishop Brian Walton's *Biblia Sacra Polyglotta,* 1657, *Tom. I, Proleg. VIII.,* and in the elder Buxtorf's *Tiberias,* printed at Basil in 1665. The general character of them will, however, be most clearly understood by the following literal translation of those pertaining to the first book of the Pentateuch, taken from Mr. W. Greenfield's meritorious work, *The Book of Genesis in English-Hebrew.* The " sign" or " symbol" which is mentioned, is a word of artificial memory, made up of letters employed as numerals, and intended to express the required number: and the passages cited indicate the precise place referred to by an initial word.

Masoretic Notes on Genesis.

The Sum of the VERSES of the Book of Genesis, is One Thousand, and Five Hundred, and Thirty and Four, אָךְלד, being its sign.

And (*the passage at*) its Half, is "And by thy sword shalt thou live" (Chap. xxvii. 40).

And its SECTIONS are Twelve, זי, "This is My Name for Ever" (*Exod.* iii. 15) being the symbol.

And its ORDERS (*Series*) are Forty and Three, מג, "Yea, and Blessed shall he be" (Chap. xxvii. 33), being the symbol.

And the CHAPTERS are Fifty, נ, "O, JEHOVAH, be gracious unto us, for THEE we have waited" (*Isaiah* xxxiii. 2), being the symbol.

The Number of the *Open Sections* is Three and Forty, מג ; and of the Close Sections Eight and Forty, מח, (*making in*) the whole Ninety and One Sections, צא צא, "Get thee out, thou and all the people that are at thy feet" (*Exod.* xi. 8, 9), being the symbol.

ADDITIONAL NOTES.

I.

All Copies of the Law must be Transcribed from Ancient Manuscripts of approved character only. Page 4.

THE Sieur De Simonville, who was one of the authors of the text illustrative of Picart's fine engravings of the Religious Ceremonies of the Jews, notices the order that synagogue copies of the Law are to be transcribed from the autograph taken by Ezra from the original written by Moses and preserved at Cairo; which, he says, "is a pure fable."—(*Cérémon. Rélig.*, i. 4, *Note C.*) But without at all attributing any manuscript to the hand of Ezra, it is quite possible that there may be some still extant which are of his time. It is evident that he employed both himself and those pious priests and Levites who are named in his interesting history, and also in that by Nehemiah, in copying and preserving those portions of the Law and the Prophets which had been transcribed under Josiah and Hilkiah, some of which it is certain were carried into Babylon at the captivity. The view which Dean Prideaux has taken of this multiplication and preservation of the Holy Scriptures, is so sagacious and interesting, that it is impossible to omit extracting it in his own words, as an important illustration of the subject of the present note.

"In the time of *Josiah*, through the impiety of the two preceding reigns of *Manasseh* and *Ammon*, the Book of the Law was so destroyed and lost, that beside that copy of it which *Hilkiah* found in the Temple there was none other to be had. For the surprise which *Hilkiah* is said to be in at the finding of it, and the grief which *Josiah* expressed at hearing it read, do plainly shew that neither of them had ever seen it before. And if the king and the high priest, who were both men of eminent piety, were without this part of Holy Scripture, it can scarcely be thought that any one else then had it. But so religious a prince as King Josiah could not leave this want long unremedied. By his order copies were forthwith written out from this original; and, search being made for all the parts of Holy Scripture,—in the colleges of the Prophets, and in all other places where they might be found,—care was taken for transcripts to be made out of these also; and thenceforth copies of the whole became multiplied among the people: all those who were desirous of knowing the Law of their God either writing them out for themselves or procuring others to do it for them. So that though within a few years after the Holy City and Temple were destroyed, and the authentic copy of the Law which was laid up before the Lord was burnt and consumed with them; yet by this time many copies both of the Law and the Prophets, and all the other sacred writings, were got into private hands who carried them with them into their captivity.

"That *Daniel* had a copy of the Holy Scriptures with him in *Babylon* it's certain, for he quotes the Law, and also makes mention of the Prophecies of the Prophet *Jeremiah* (*Dan.* ix. 2, 11, 13), which he could not do if he had never seen them. And in the sixth chapter of *Ezra* it is said, that on the finishing of the Temple, in the sixth year of *Darius*, the priests and Levites were settled in their respective functions, *according as it is written in the Law of Moses*; but how could they do this according to the written Law, if they had not copies of that Law then among them? And *this was nearly sixty years before Ezra came to Jerusalem*. And farther, in the eighth chapter of *Nehemiah*, when the people called for the Law of *Moses*, to have it read to them, they did not pray Ezra to get it anew dictated unto him, but that he should *bring forth* the Book of the Law of *Moses*, which the Lord had commanded to *Israel*; which plainly shews that the book was then well known to have been extant."—*Connection of the History of the Old and New Testament*, 1720. Part I., Book v., p. 260.

By the time of the destruction of the Second Temple, the whole number of the sacred rolls preserved there, and throughout all the provincial synagogues, must have been very considerable. Dr. Kennicott, on the authority of Wolfius and of a certain Jew, named Moses Pereyra, states that about eighty of the Jews, who had escaped from Titus, travelled through Persia to the coast of Malabar; where Pereyra found some manuscript copies of the Hebrew text. There are, however, very few *really ancient exemplars known to be extant*; and Dr. Kennicott supposed that almost all the Hebrew manuscripts of his time were written between the years 1000 and 1147. He concludes with Bishop Walton, that those which were written before A. D. 700 or 800 were destroyed by some order of the Jewish Senate, on account of their many variations from the copies then considered to be genuine. The learned Jews who came into Europe in the beginning of the eleventh century, brought with them transcripts from authentic manuscripts, some of which were pointed; and in the two following centuries other copies were made with greater care than was exercised in succeeding ages. In making those copies the transcribers followed certain exemplars, eight in number, which were highly esteemed for their accuracy, as the standard texts. They are now lost, but extracts from them are still preserved; and from Jewish writings, and the margins of some manuscripts, it is ascertained that they were highly prized for their singular accuracy. They were known by the names of " *The Codex of Hillel*; " " *The Codex of Ben Asher*," called also " *The Palestine, Jerusalem, or Egyptian Codex*; " " *The Codex of Ben Naphtali*," or " *The Babylonian Codex*; " " *The Codex of Jericho*; " " *The Codex of Sinai*; " and " *The Book Taggin*."

II.

Parchment prepared by a Jew from the Skin of a clean Animal. Page 4.

THE skins which might be employed for this purpose, were those of the calf, the sheep, the kid, and the goat; and the oldest Hebrew Rolls which are now known to exist are supposed to be those written on leather made of goat-skins dyed red. In the year 1806, Dr. Claudius Buchanan discovered such a Roll of the Pentateuch, 48 feet in length, in the record-chest of a synagogue of black Jews in the interior of Malayala. This he bought, and it is now deposited in the Public Library of the University of Cambridge. The Cabul Jews, who travel annually into the interior of China, report that in some synagogues there, also, the Law is to be found written on soft flexible leather made of the same material. It is a very remarkable circumstance, and one which never could have been imagined without indisputable proof, that *any* community of Jews should be permitted to dispose of the Sacred Books belonging to their synagogue; but it has been shewn, on a previous page, that the *Mishna* evidently recognises the act as lawful, and only directs the purposes for which the proceeds are to be employed.

III.

Every Membrane must contain a certain Number of Columns of prescribed Dimensions, each consisting of a certain Number of Lines and Words. Page 4.

It is considered that in the best Hebrew Rolls the columns should not exceed in breadth half their length; and these columns must all be of the same dimensions, and contain the same number of lines, quite filled up with complete words. In consequence of this accuracy and the beauty of the penmanship, the synagogue copies of the Law have always been very much admired. The Père Richard Simon, from whose works was compiled the Second Dissertation prefixed to the engravings of Picart, says of these Rolls, " I should not have found anything to detract from the exact precision which characterises the small pages or columns of those volumes which are intended for synagogues, if it were not to be attributed to superstition; instead of which it is evident that the dimensions were really appointed to render these Rolls more proportionate and beautiful."—(*Cérémon. Relig.*, i. p. 54.)

After the short notices which have been already given of the rigid rules to be observed in transcribing the Law, it would not be supposed that the examiners of a copy would allow of *three mistakes on one skin, or four in the whole volume:* but if the Song of the Deliverance at the Red Sea, or that uttered by Moses at the time of his death, were to be written close instead of being displayed as poetry, the error would vitiate the manuscript. In the Talmud are contained all the established regulations relating to the materials of a Roll; the ink, the pen, the letters, the divisions, and all the other peculiarities which are required to be closely adhered to, especially in the transcription of the Pentateuch. They are likewise to be found translated from the Hebrew, in Dr. James George Christian Adler's work, entitled *"Judæorum Codices Sacri Ritè Scribendi Leges, ad recte æstimandos Codices Manuscriptos antiquos per veteres,"* published at Hamburg in 1779.

Although the plain square Hebrew character, without points, is that which is directed to be always used for the writing of Rolls of the Law, yet even in those copied out for synagogues, it is still recognised as having some varieties. One of them is called the *Tam* letter, which is known by its sharp corners and perpendicular coronulæ, and it is used by the German and Polish Jews; and the other, which is rounder and more modern, is employed by the Jews of Spain and Portugal, and is called *Velsha*. The peculiar angularity of the letters in the Roll described in the previous pages, no doubt indicates that it is written in the *Tam* character, though most probably in Holland.

IV.

The Columns are numbered for every Book separately. Page 6.

THE leaves mentioned in the authorised English translation of the Prophecy of Jeremiah, xxxvi. 23, and the "*pagella*" of the Vulgate version, are really the columns of a Hebrew Roll. The original word is דְּלָתוֹת, *Delithuth*, or doors; because the pages of books are like doors or gates in admitting to the sense, as this passage is explained by the Rabbi Elias. These columns likewise appear to be referred to by St. Luke, iv. 17, where he relates that Jesus Christ went into the synagogue at Nazareth "on the Sabbath Day, and stood up for to read—and there was delivered unto Him the Book of the Prophet Esaias. And when *He had opened the book, He found the place where it is written*," etc. Dr. Lightfoot considers that the Roll was given to Him by "the minister of the church who kept the Sacred Books in his custody, and brought them out to be read when they met together in the synagogue. The words, therefore, of our Evangelist, Ἀναπτύξας τὸ βιβλίον, to me seem not barely to mean that He unfolded or opened the book, but that, being opened, He unrolled it from folio to folio, until He had found the place which He designed to read and expound." (*Works*, 1684. ii. p. 407, 408, *Hebrew and Talmudical Exercitations*.) In reading the Law in the synagogue, it was not permissible for the reader to unroll from one passage to another, but this might be done with the books of the Prophets: and, therefore, though Christ *might* not have taken the section appointed for the particular day, He did not violate any established order, not to speak of the power of His divine authority.

It is doubtful, however, as Dean Alford observes, "whether the Rabbinical cycle of Sabbath readings, or lessons from the Law and the Prophets, were yet in use; but some regular plan was adopted, and, according to that plan, after the reading of the Law, which always preceded, the portion from the Prophets came to be read (*See Acts*, xiii. 15), which, for that Sabbath, fell in the Prophet Isaiah. The Roll containing that book, probably that alone, was given to the Lord, but it does not appear that He read any part of the lesson for the day; but when He had unrolled the scroll, '*found*'—the *fortuitous, id est the providential*, finding, is the most likely interpretation,—not the searching for, and finding—the passage which follows. No inference can be drawn as to the time of the year from this narrative; partly on account of the uncertainty above-mentioned, and partly because it is not quite clear whether the Roll contained only Isaiah, or other books also." (*The Greek Testament*, vol. i. 1854, *p.* 431, *Note* 17.)

In this sense of *simply opening and finding*, the Greek word is used more than once by Euripides: but that the passage in question really was the Scripture for the day, appears to be almost proved by the very nature of a Hebrew Roll, and the custom which is still observed in the synagogues with regard to

ADDITIONAL NOTES.

the Book of the Law. In closing the volume, the person whose peculiar duty it is to shut it and to fold it up, should bring the two rolls together, at the place where the reader left off on one day, and was to commence on the next: for which arrangement the Hebrew double rolls were adapted beyond any other form of book ever known. The conclusion, therefore, seems to be almost unavoidable, that when Christ *opened* the book, *He naturally found or discovered* the prophecy which follows. In His divine knowledge of all things, He went up to the synagogue of Nazareth *designedly* on the day when that especial Scripture ought to be read; and, like His apostle Philip, when discoursing from the same Prophet, He began " at the same Scripture, and preached unto them Jesus."

It may, however, be objected, in reply to this conjecture, that even the Synagogue rolls containing the writings of the Prophets, were not *double*, like those of The Law, and therefore were probably not folded up in the same manner; but this is a question involving a matter of ancient practice, which cannot now be answered. Almost the only positive information extant on the subject is contained in the Prophesies of Jeremiah and Habakuk. In chapter xxxvi. 2, 32, of the former Prophet, he is directed to take "*a Roll of a Book*;" and the original compound word מְגִלַּת־סֵפֶר *meguillath sepher*, signifies no more than the single volume expressed by the English translation; but this might be rolled together from both ends, and so be opened at the place referred to by St. Luke. In the modern synagogues the rolls are of The Law only, the other Sacred Books being square manuscripts; but it will be evident, from the preceding part of this note, that there cannot be any question that the Scripture given to Jesus Christ in the Synagogue at Nazareth was really a roll, whether it were single or double.

V.

When these Offices become vacant, the privilege of performing them is offered to public Auction in the Synagogue by one of the Clerks. Page 15.

BUXTORF's account of these sales, as they existed in Germany in the seventeenth century, is so remarkably curious and characteristic, and is probably so little known in the original form, that a translation of the whole passage is here inserted from the author's very rare work *Synagoga Judaica. Basil*, 1661, 8vo. c. xxvii. p. 543.

" Because the Reading of the Law is finished on this day—*the 23d of Tishri, which occurs towards the end of September*—it is called THE REJOICING OF THE LAW: and those funds which arise out of the sale of the honour and privilege of reading the Law, and which are purely ecclesiastical and especially belonging to the synagogue, are then forthwith to be replenished. These offices are also publicly sold in the synagogue, in the manner of an auction; and they are disposed of to such persons as will give the most for them after three special proclamations have been previously made for each.

" The first privilege which is announced by the warden or clerk, is that of lighting certain lamps in the synagogue for the whole year. Next follows the duty of supplying the wine which is consecrated and distributed on the

Sabbath and other feast days; and it is accordingly submitted for valuation. But all the fathers of families ought as a duty to offer 'the Sabbath wine' as a gift to the poor Jews who have not any; since it is an established obligation, and is decreed to all such as delight in and honour the Sabbath to consecrate and to distribute one cup of wine to their households. They give the wine even to children, but this act is avoided by some of the more pious Jews.

"Thirdly is proclaimed, 'What is to be the price of the office which is called גלילת?' namely, *Gelilath*, or the Right of Covering: that is, the duty of unbinding and tying up again the Books of the Law. Fourthly is demanded, 'Who will be the הגבהה?' or the *Hagbahah*; whose office is to take the Book of the Law when it is laid open, and to hold it upright on high, turning and shewing it to all around, that every one may see the writing. The buyer of this duty ought to be a strong and stout person, who *can* hold the book, even when it is a large one, opened and stretched out with his arms extended to shew it to the congregation; for if it should fall to the ground, or his foot should stumble, it would be required that the whole synagogue should fast to expiate such an unhappy omen.

"Fifthly it is asked, 'Who will buy עץ היים?' meaning *Ost hajim*, or the Trees of Life: which is the privilege of turning round those two wooden rollers, to which are attached the skins whereon the Law is written; taking hold of them, and of the linen covers belonging to them, and rolling them out, and also of afterwards rolling them up again. This privilege is commonly sold to some of the younger persons of the synagogue, for they suppose that their holding up of these two pieces of wood will be followed by their becoming wiser and better: and they hope also to procure by them a long life, because they are called עץ היים *Ost Hajim*, or the Wood of Lives: for it is written in *Proverbs* iii., 'She is a Tree of Life to all that lay hold upon her.' Whilst the book is closed and tied up, it is held by the wooden handles only; and if it were to be touched by the naked hand the offender would commit a great crime, which would require a very solemn expiation.

"Sixthly is proclaimed, 'Who is willing to give the price of אחרון?' or *Acherun*: which is the privilege of being called up to perform the Reading of the Book of the Law at Festivals; and this also is sold to the last bidder out of the whole assembly. Seventhly is cried, 'Who desireth in his heart to become שהייה?' or *Schehijah*: which is the honour of being considered sufficient to execute the office of any one of the other officers who might neglect his duty, or not carefully perform it. The money which is raised by these sales is employed for the repairs of the synagogue, and the benefit of the poor belonging to it." Buxtorf proceeds to state that much hostility, envy, and quarrelling, were excited by the equality and competition of all ranks at these sales.

VI.
"*The Cloth of the Quintanes.*" Page 17.

The whole passage, as it appears in Dr. Lightfoot's *Hebrew and Talmudical Exercitations on the Evangelist St. Luke*, iv. 17, *Works*, 1684, II. p. 407, is so remarkably interesting and curious, that it is inserted entire in this note.

"All do know what title the Books of the Law do bear in the front of our Hebrew Bibles, namely, חמשה חומשי התורה, *Hamishe Humishi Hathorah* —The five Quintanes (or Fifths) of the Law : Genesis is חומש ראשון, *Humish Rashin,* the First Quintane (or Fifth Part); Exodus is חומש שני, *Humish Sheni,* the Second Quintane.

"They fold up the Book of the Law in the Cloth of the Quintanes, and the Quintanes in the Cloth of the Prophets and the *Hagiographa*; but they do not fold up the Prophets and the *Hagiographa* in the Cloth of the Quintanes, nor the (*separate*) Quintanes in the Cloth of the (*whole*) Law. They lay the (*entire*) Law על הומשין, *Ol Humishin,* upon the (*separate*) Quintanes, and the Quintanes upon the Prophets and the *Hagiographa*; but not the Prophets and *Hagiographa* upon the Quintanes, nor the (*separate*) Quintanes upon the (*whole*) Law; that is, *not any one single Quintane, upon all the Quintanes made up into one volume.* A QUINTANE is a Book of the Law, in which there is but one Quintane."

VII.

In the Side, or By the Side of the Ark. Page 18.

It seems to have been Dr. Kennicott who first observed that the words in *Deuteronomy,* xxxi. 26, וְשַׂמְתֶּם אֹתוֹ מִצַּד אֲרוֹן *Vaishmathim athu matzod Aron,* translated in the authorised English version, "put it *in* the side of the ark," really signified *by the side of it*; that is, that the *original* book might always be ready, as an indisputable authority on any occasion of high importance without the ark being touched. Even *within the vail,* the passage to the ark and the mercy-seat was restricted and closed up by the staves by which the ark was carried, between which the high priest entered once in the year, only on the Day of Expiation. But by the Book of the Law being placed *by the side of the ark without,* it might be taken up and returned by the high priest passing his hand only behind the curtain, without his committing the violation of entering the sanctuary.

II.

The Masorites and Masoretic Notes.

The religious observance of the traditional regulations of the Jews for so many centuries in copying The Law, have been frequently commended, as having proved to be of the greatest value in preserving the purity of the text. But this effect was most importantly increased, at the introduction of that extraordinary system of numerical analysis of the written words, invented by the *later* Masorists. In the history of Hebrew Literature there appear to have been two parties of teachers, to each of which the title of a Masoretic school properly belonged; though they existed at very different periods, and had really different objects of study and instruction.

ADDITIONAL NOTES.

Dr. Etheridge has given the best account of the early Masorists, in his interesting and elaborate little volume on the history of Hebrew Literature; in which he states that " their labours were restricted within the field of Scripture and Tradition. Their studies," he continues, " turned upon the Canonical documents themselves, and such, in their view, *authentic traditions* as contributed to fix their meaning, and to ramify their application to the various interests of life and the solemnities of religion. The men of this school built entirely on authority. They believed nothing, and taught nothing, but what they had *received*. Hence came their distinctive title of *Masorists*, from *Masr*—Traderi, *veluti de manu in manum*." The time when they flourished seems to have been about 300 years B.C., and they are to be distinguished from the school of the Philosophic Jews, which was contemporaneous, by their devoting themselves to the *Letter* of the Law; whereas the latter so endeavoured to understand the *Spirit* of it, as to extract therefrom the principles of Universal Truth, or a Sacred Philosophy.

But the efforts of both these schools tended most materially to spread an intimate knowledge of the Holy Scriptures, as contained in the Pentateuch, and to preserve a minute purity of the text: and their researches appear to have been continued at a much later period by the MASORITES and CABALISTS, who became their representatives. By both of these bodies of Teachers, TRADITION was held to be the one great element of instruction:—by the first as *delivering down* an uncorrupted text, pure even to the very letters; and by the second as *receiving* from it those mystical doctrines which were anciently developed and taught as existing in all its sentences and character. Early in the sixth century A. D., the Rabbins of the pre-eminent school at Tiberias were engaged in preparing an accurate edition of the Holy Scriptures in Hebrew; and to them is now attributed the insertion of the smaller sub-divisions of the ancient large portions appointed for daily reading. The *Sedarim*, or series, with some kind of separation into short verses, must have been regulated by Ezra and his colleagues, nearly a thousand years before this time; and it was admirably fitted for the common-people of the Jews. But, with the expectation of certifying, and of unalterably securing the text of the Holy volume,—the later Masorists counted the number of verses in all the books:—they ascertained also the middle verse and letter in each, with the number of their letters. These have been estimated to amount to 815,280: but it is considered that this is only an approximation to the real number. The Masorites also counted the repetition of every character of the Hebrew Alphabet; and also noted down many other precise and curious particulars.

Printed by Libri Plureos GmbH in Hamburg,
Germany